Pioneer Life

Frontier American Activity Book

Typography Lorraine Stegman	**Author** Linda Milliken
Illustrations Barb Lorseyedi	

METRIC CONVERSION CHART

Refer to this chart when metric conversions are not found within the activity.

¼ tsp	= 1 ml	1 oz.	= 28 g	350° F	= 180° C	1 inch	= 2.54 cm	¼ cup	60 ml
½ tsp	= 2 ml	1 lb.	= .45 kg	375° F	= 190° C	1 foot	= 30 cm	⅓ cup	= 80 ml
1 tsp	= 5 ml			400° F	= 200° C	1 yard	= 91 cm	½ cup	= 125 ml
1 Tbsp	= 15 ml			425° F	= 216° C	1 mile	= 1.6 km	1 cup	= 250 ml

©1990 **Edupress, Inc.** • P.O. Box 883 • Dana Point, CA 92629

ISBN 1-56472-017-9
Printed in USA

Trail Map Activities

Follow along with the pioneers as they travel west. Here are two choices for mapping the routes westward. Choose one or both!

Individual Trail Map

Reproduce the map pages, following. Glue the pages together in the center, overlapping, to create one large map.

As students complete the trail activities that follow they can track their progress westward. Use a different colored marker or crayon for each trail. Color the landmarks as you pass.

Select other map activities appropriate to student abilities:

• Add geographic features. Research these features.
Through what future states did the pioneers travel?
What is the highest elevation of the Appalachian Mountains? The Rockies?

• Many pioneers, if they could write, kept a journal of their daily progress. Students can write their own journals about their wagon trip west. Was it hot? What did they see? What exciting (or boring) events took place? How many miles were traveled that day?

Large-Scale Trail Map

Use yarn to recreate a huge outline of the United States on a classroom wall. Students add geographic features using construction paper. Use a different color yarn for each trail. Keep track of your westward progress by tacking signs and pictures to note the location of each landmark. Tack up the student-made prairie schooners along the trails. Group some in Independence, getting ready to head out.

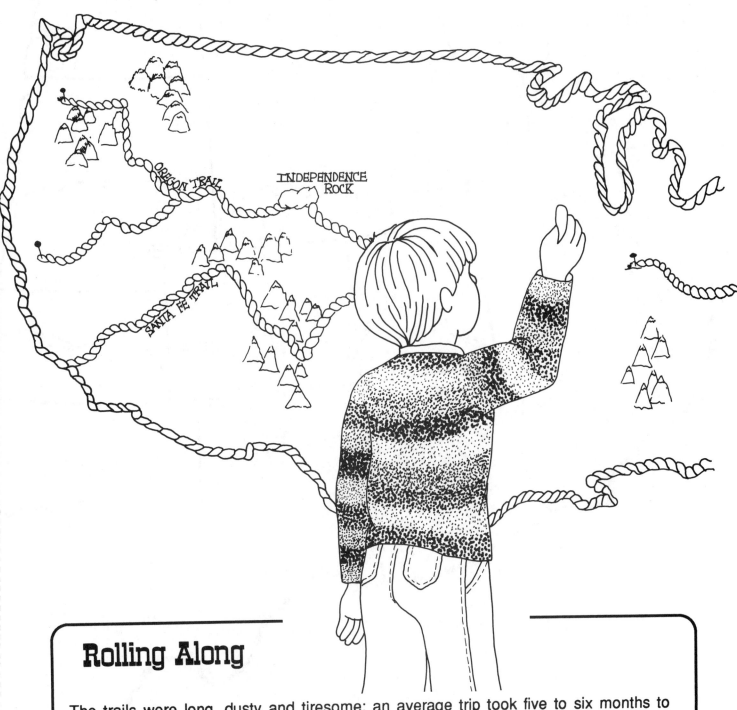

Rolling Along

The trails were long, dusty and tiresome; an average trip took five to six months to complete. Danger and hardships were part of daily life. But the sights were also spectacular as you will learn as you "travel" each trail.

VANCOUVER

OREGON TRAIL

CALIFORNIA TRAIL

SACRAMENTO

OREGON TRAIL

OLD SPANISH TRAIL

SANTA FE TRAIL

OLD SPANISH TRAIL

LOS ANGELES

Santa Fe

CUMBERLAND

INDEPENDENCE

You Can't Take It With You

Historical Aid: Pioneers heading west had to know what things to take and what to leave behind. Certain equipment was necessary for the journey and building a new frontier home. The earliest pioneers took only what they could carry or load on horseback. Families traveling by wagon packed what fit into this 5 foot by 10 foot space!

Most pioneers took along a hammer, saw, hoe and plow for basic building and farming. Household goods consisted of a few pots and pans, iron kettle, blankets and perhaps a spinning wheel. Many took only the clothes they wore. They also packed sacks of corn meal and salt and dried beef. A lantern, compass and rope were valuable possessions. A rifle and ammunition were important for survival. Few luxuries were taken; if room permitted a clock and a Bible were packed.

Many keepsakes, family treasures and valuable objects were left behind. These were difficult choices for the pioneers to make but they knew that the things needed for survival were the most important possessions of all on the frontier.

It's decision-making time for all classroom pioneers heading west on a wagon trip.

Give students a large piece of construction paper and a copy of the following page. Fold the paper in half. Label one half "TAKE" and the other half "LEAVE."

Color and cut out the items on the picture page. Children decide which items to take and which to leave behind and paste them on the correct half of the paper. Older students can number their choices in order of importance.

Remember, everything must fit into a covered wagon. Measure a five by ten foot area in the classroom so the children have an idea of the available packing space. Compare and discuss their choices.

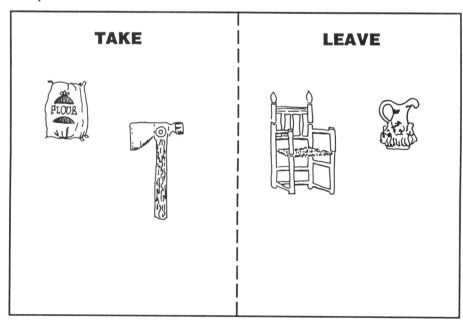

Historical Aid: The first pioneers heading west walked or rode on horseback. They followed trails previously made by buffalo and deer. Giant trees were everywhere. There were so many scarcely a patch of sunlight shone through the trees onto the forest floor.

When wagons began to roll west these giant trees had to be cut to clear a trail. This was hard, backbreaking work. Not much distance was travelled in a day's journey.

Early Trails

Recreate the towering trees and dense forest through which the early pioneers traveled.

You will need *heavy construction paper, crayons, yellow paint* and *brushes.*

Here's what to do:

1. Cover the paper with heavily-colored green trees.
2. Add brown trunks and the forest floor.
3. Paint with a wash of yellow tempera or watercolors.

Cumberland Road

Historical Aid: The first trail west through the Appalachian Mountains was the Cumberland Gap. This natural pass began at the meeting point of Virginia, Kentucky and Tennessee. Its narrow steep sides led the way for 200,000 pioneers between 1775 and 1800.

Daniel Boone (see People and Places section) was hired to clear another trail through the pass. This was called both the Wilderness Road and the Cumberland Road. It led from Cumberland, Maryland to Vandalia, Illinois.

Blazing the trail was backbreaking work. Much of it was done with an ax and the strong arms of daring woodsmen.

Prepare to blaze The Cumberland Road. You'll need an ax!

- Roll a length of construction paper several times to make a sturdy handle. Tape to hold.

- Use the pattern to cut two ax blades from lightweight cardboard. Staple them to both sides of one tube end. Glue the blades together and cover with foil.

Head outside with your axes and blaze a trail through bushes of crumpled newspaper.

Wagons Ho

Historical Aid: As time passed wagons began to follow the foot and horse trails leading west. Two types of wagons were most commonly used.

The **Conestoga**, sometimes called the *camel of the prairie*, hauled freight and people across the Alleghenies for over 100 years. Its wheels were high so the body cleared tree stumps. The ends tilted up so the weight of the cargo stayed in the middle. When the wheels were removed the wagon doubled as a boat. The Conestoga was first built by the Pennsylvania Dutch who painted the body blue and the gear bright red. A team of four to six horses pulled the wagon.

The **Prairie Schooner** was home for families and their belongings traveling to Oregon and California. The wagon was called a prairie schooner because, from a distance, its white top looked like the sails of a ship. It was a standard farm wagon with very sturdy wheels. Not built for comfort, many travelers found it easier to walk than ride.

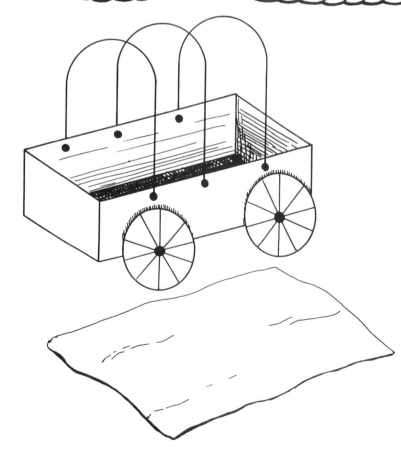

Shoebox Conestoga

• Remove the lid and paint a shoebox blue. When the blue paint dries paint red trim.

• Cut four large wheels from cardboard and attach them with brads to the sides of the box.

• Poke wire or pipe cleaners through the box at three points (see illustration). Curve the wire and fasten to the box on the opposite side.

• Cut a piece of white material or construction paper the length of the box and wide enough to cover the wire. Glue in place.

Wagons Ho!

Personalized Prairie Schooner

Many families traveling west wrote messages on the white canvas stretched across the top of their wagons. These messages often shared the family's final destination and expressed hope and enthusiasm for the journey ahead. Some messages read:

On to Nebraska

California or Bust

Bound for Oregon

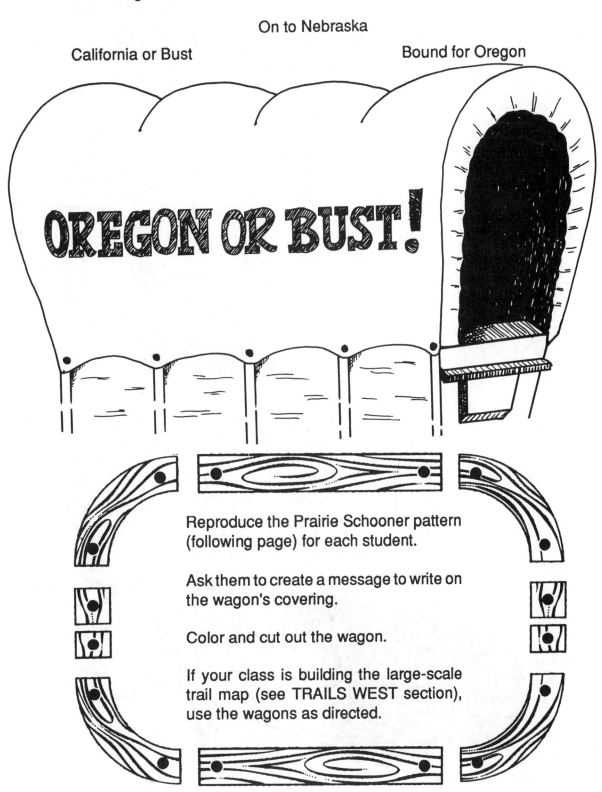

Reproduce the Prairie Schooner pattern (following page) for each student.

Ask them to create a message to write on the wagon's covering.

Color and cut out the wagon.

If your class is building the large-scale trail map (see TRAILS WEST section), use the wagons as directed.

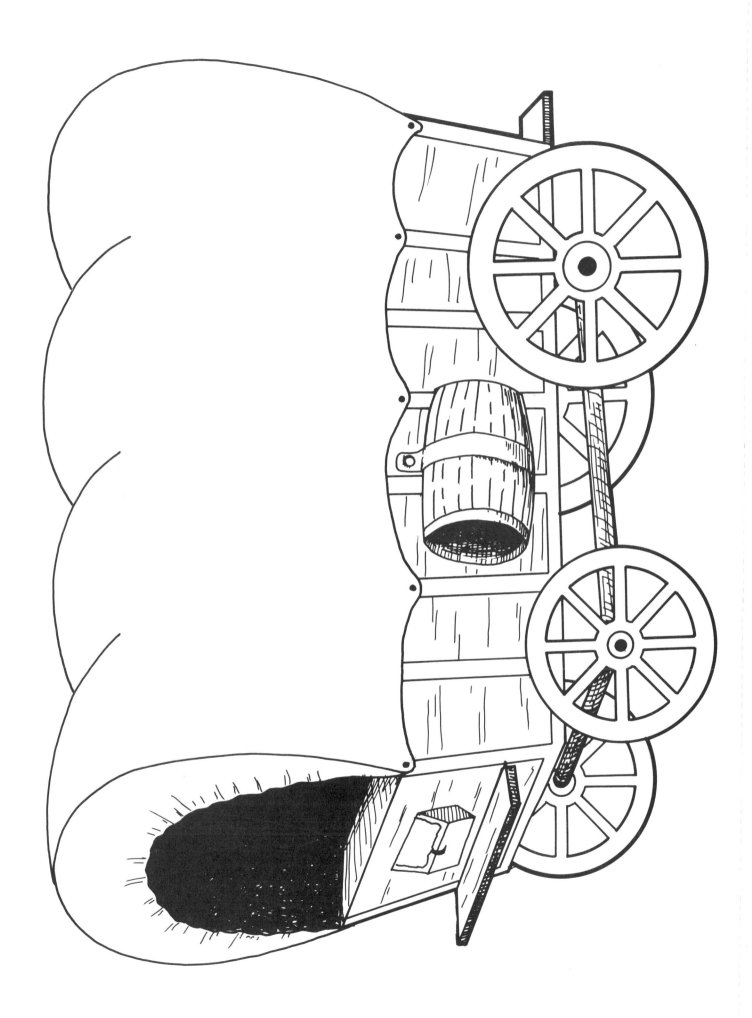

Wagon Trains West

Historical Aid: Wagon trains with as many as a hundred families gathered in and departed from Independence, Missouri, bound for the far western frontier. They chose either the Oregon Trail heading northwest or the Santa Fe Trail, heading southwest.

Wagons were on the trail by early spring to avoid harsh winter weather. Before the train left Independence, officers were elected. Their decisions along the trail were law. Wagons were grouped in two divisions, each with a captain. Both divisions were subdivided into platoons of four wagons each. A scout and a wagon master were hired to lead the way, select camp sites and act as advisors.

Before your students head their wagons west, follow the same procedures as the pioneers.

Elect officers, divide into divisions and platoons, select a scout and a wagon master.

TRAIL LAWS
1. NO STEALING WATER OR FOOD
2. NO SHOOTING GUN WHILE MOVING
3. NO BRAWLING
4.

Work in subdivisions of about four students to write some laws for the people on the wagon train. Remember to keep in mind some of the troubles that might arise—fighting, lack of water, Indian attacks, weather conditions.

Write these laws on parchment (butcher paper) and post them for all to see. Compare the laws the committees created.

Oregon Trail

This was the longest of the overland routes used by the pioneers, winding over 2,000 miles through prairies and deserts and across mountains. The trail headed through Kansas and Nebraska and along the Platte River. Food, water and wood were scarce. The Trail ended with a journey down the Columbia River to the Willamette Valley in Oregon.

This Way to Oregon

Not many miles out of Independence, the wagons encountered a road sign. It said, "Oregon Trail." This simple sign was hardly any indication of the difficult journey that lay ahead!

Project: Oregon Trail Road Sign

Crumple a brown shopping bag and tear or cut it into the shape shown.

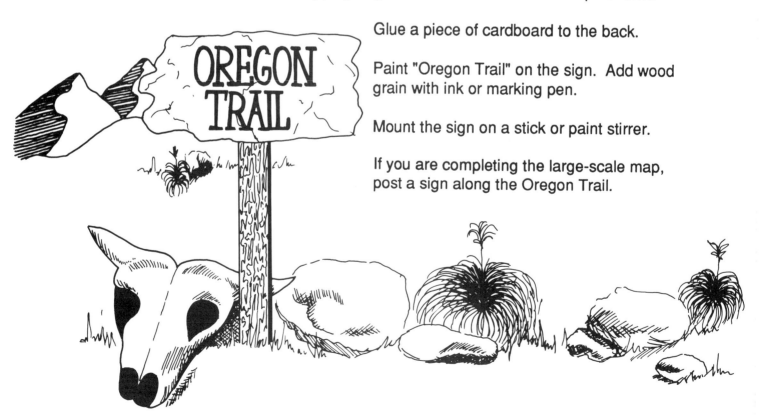

Glue a piece of cardboard to the back.

Paint "Oregon Trail" on the sign. Add wood grain with ink or marking pen.

Mount the sign on a stick or paint stirrer.

If you are completing the large-scale map, post a sign along the Oregon Trail.

Chimney Rock

The first major geographic landmark the pioneers encountered along the Oregon Trail was Chimney Rock. The spire of Chimney Rock rises about 500 feet above the Platte River enabling the pioneers to see it from miles away.

Project: Recreate Chimney Rock

Paint a background on white paper. Include the Platte River.

When the background paint has dried glue pieces of crumpled tissue paper in shades of white, yellow and brown to form the shape of Chimney Rock as shown in the illustration.

Independence Rock

This huge block of granite, 650 yards long, is on the north bank of the Sweetwater River near Alcova, Wyoming. It is called Independence Rock because all wagon trains tried to reach this point before the fourth of July. That meant good progress was being made. One traveler said the rock reminded him of a "huge whale" rising above the plains. Hundreds of pioneers scratched their name on Independence Rock before continuing on their journey.

Project: Recreate Independence Rock

Sketch a large rock on construction paper. Place a sheet of waxed paper, waxy side down, over the construction paper. Ask pioneer classmates to write their names on the waxed paper. Remove the waxed paper and paint over the rock with a watercolor wash. The names of the pioneers will appear as if scratched out over a century ago!

California Trail

Historical Aid: The California Trail branched off from the Oregon Trail and headed southwest 800 miles through the Rockies and Sierra Nevada Mountains. The route was a treacherous climb. No time could be lost as the wagon trains were in a race with the potential of an early winter's snow to get to their final destination—Sacramento, California.

Create a dimensional picture of a wagon heading across the Rockies on the California Trail.

- Paint a mountainous background on a large sheet of white construction paper. Allow to dry.

- Paint and cut out a reproduced copy of the Prairie Schooner Pattern (page 12).

- Glue three small sponge pieces in a triangular pattern to the back of the Prairie Schooner. Then apply glue to the sponge pieces and mount the wagon to the background paper.

- Sponge paint or Q-tip paint white tempera "snow" over the picture and wagon.

Exploring Some More

Find out about the ill-fated Donner Party and the fascinating tale of their wagon journey along the California Trail and over the Sierra Nevada Mountains.

Santa Fe Trail

Historical Aid: The Santa Fe Trail opened in 1821 and was used for 60 years. It stretched nearly 1,000 miles from Franklin, Missouri to Santa Fe, New Mexico. The trail cut across prairie, mountain and desert. It had two branches. The northern branch was difficult for wagon travel. The southern branch was shorter but had no source for water.

The Santa Fe Trail was mainly used as a commercial route. Traders took manufactured goods to Santa Fe to exchange for mules, furs, gold and silver with the Spanish inhabitants.

Wagon Mound

This was a familiar landmark to passing travelers. Its shape seemed to resemble a Prairie Schooner. When a pioneer reached Wagon Mound he knew Santa Fe was only 100 miles beyond.

• Make a pen and ink sketch of Wagon Mound.

• Look on a map of your state. What cities and towns are 100 miles from where you live?

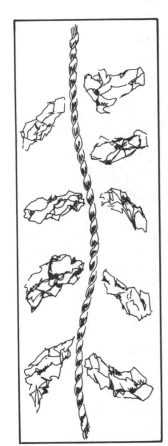

On to Santa Fe

This 200-year-old Spanish colonial city was a major destination for those traveling the Santa Fe Trail. Upon arriving, weary travelers were greeted by the colorful sight of ristas (strings) of chili peppers in the hot sun.

Brighten the classroom with these chili peppers:
• Glue yarn down the center of a 4" x 18" strip of manila construction paper.

• At intervals on each side of the yarn, glue a chili pepper-shaped piece of crumpled red tissue paper.

Prickly Sights

Historical Aid: As the pioneers traveled west there was a great change in the landscape from what they were used to in their eastern homes.

The trail was dusty and dry. One of the strangest new plants the pioneers encountered was the cactus plant which is found in great abundance.

These plants shed their leaves and make food in their stems. Most cactus plants are protected by sharp bristles and spines that protect it against animals that live in the desert. The pioneers found many uses for these unusual plants.

There are many different types of cactus. Make a *mini-mural* of cactus the pioneers might have seen as they traveled west.

Here's what to do:
Fold a large piece of white construction paper into 4 sections. "Grow" a different cactus in each. Use the illustrations and information on the next page as a guide. Label each and write a fact about the cactus.

  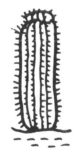 

Exploring Some More

* Make a list of as many different kinds of cactus as you can find. Tell an interesting fact about each.

* Grow cactus plants in class.

* Research the different uses of cactus. Make a chart.

* Learn about the plant "aloe." What are its benefits?

Giant Cactus

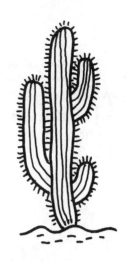

Fact: This cactus may reach a height of 50 feet. It is the largest of all the cactus in the United States. It produces a fruit that can be eaten fresh or made into preserves.

Art: Color or paint a giant cactus. Sponge paint yellow blooms on the tip of each branch.

Barrel Cactus

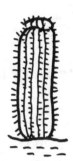

Fact: This cactus has tough, curved spines that Indians once used as fishhooks. The juicy pulp saved the life of many thirsty travelers.

Art: Color a brown oval with yellow flowers growing out the top. Use a felt-tipped marker to make curved spines.

Prickly Pear

Fact: This cactus has thorny, leaflike stems. It bears pear-shaped fruit that is good to eat.

Art: Draw several oval-shaped, pale green leaves. Glue toothpicks to resemble thorns.

Old Man

Fact: This cactus has a shaggy coat of white hair that protects it from the sun. It has no thorns.

Art: Draw a "dill pickle" shape. Paint or color it yellow. Glue cornsilk or thinly shredded yellow tissue over the cactus.

Old Spanish Trail

Historical Aid: The Old Spanish Trail was an extension of the Santa Fe Trail. It ran from Santa Fe, New Mexico to Los Angeles, California by way of Durango, Colorado, along the Colorado River and across the Mohave desert. While not one of the more dangerous trails the route, nevertheless, was parched and lacked an abundant water supply.

Along the way travelers saw the buttes, mesas, peaks and valleys that make up the desert. The setting sun was welcome relief from the hot sun that beat upon the wagon travelers all day.

Recreate the silhouette of a wagon against a desert sunset.

- Watercolor several bands of color—blue, lavendar, yellow, rust and red—horizontally across a sheet of white construction paper.

- When dry, create a desert scene by cutting out black paper shapes and gluing them to the watercolor backdrop.

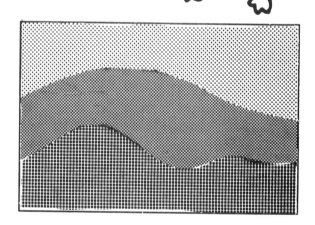

Try adding all or some of these shapes:
    wagon
    cactus
    mesas
    coyote

This Land is My Land

Historical Aid: The western frontier was first inhabited by the Indians. In an attempt to protect themselves and their land the Indians attacked the wagon trains from time to time.

Forts were built along the trails to serve not only as a trading post and resting spot but also as protection against hostile Indian attacks. Some famous frontier forts were Boonesville (built and named by Daniel Boone), Bridger, Laramie, Sutter's and McKenzie.

Craft (popsicle) sticks can be used to recreate these two important sights on the western frontier.

Fort

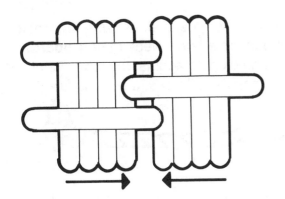

Build fence sections with the **craft sticks**. Lay two sticks horizontally about two inches apart.

Glue sticks side by side on the horizontal sticks. Connect sections by overlapping horizontal sticks (see illustration).

Use **heavy cardboard** as a base. Press the fence sections into strips of **clay** to hold in place.

A **quart milk carton** can be covered to place in one corner of the fort to serve as a watch tower.

Indian Teepee Village

Use the **craft sticks** to **glue** three upside down "V" shapes on manila or white **construction paper**.

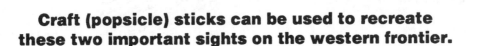

Draw Indian symbols inside the upside down V shape.

Paint a background.

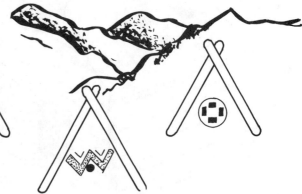

Frontier Homes

Historical Aid: The homes on the frontier, from the Appalachians in the east to the Rockies in the west, were as varied as the settlers themselves. People needed shelter and the pioneers had to make do with what they found in the wilderness.

Divide into groups, or choose individually, and build models of frontier homes.

Lean-to

Settlers needed temporary shelter before winter weather arrived. They built a structure called a **lean-to**, or a **half-camp**. It was three-sided, facing away from the wind. The open side faced a fire that burned night and day. The back wall was often a large, fallen log. The remaining sides and roof were built from twisted bark and branches.

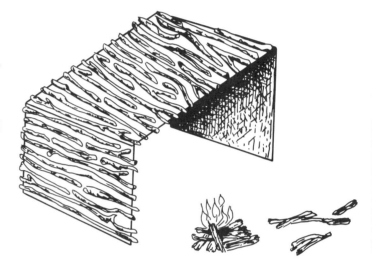

■ To build a lean-to you will need a **paper tube**, **box** (with two opposite sides cut out), **brown paint**, **small sticks** and **twigs**, and **glue**. Build the model on a large piece of **cardboard**. Begin by gluing the tube to the cardboard. Set one open box side against the tube. Paint the box. Glue sticks and twigs to the remaining sides. Add detail—tall trees, a burning fire, animals.

When spring arrived, Appalachian pioneers were able to cut down trees, shape the wood into logs and build a log cabin. Neighbors helped each other with the job of lifting the heavy logs. The ends of the logs were notched to lock together. A chimney was built on one wall. Window openings were sometimes covered with animal skin or oiled paper but usually were uncovered.

■ Roll **paper** logs. **Glue** them on top of each other to form a four-sided house. Add a **construction paper** chimney. Leave openings for windows and door. Roof with folded construction paper.

Log Cabin

The farmers on the great plains built dirt homes called **soddies.** Furrows of sod were plowed and cut into blocks one-foot square. Blocks were piled in rows to make walls and covered with a thatched roof. The soddies were sometimes improved by hauling in lumber for doors and ceilings and whitewashing the walls.

Soddy

■ Shape **self-hardening clay** into one-inch blocks. Stack to create the four walls, moistening the rows to hold them together. Paint with a thin, **white tempera** wash. Add a **paper** roof covered with **dried grass**.

Texas Ranch House

A **ranch house** consisted of two log cabins joined by an open, roofed space. One side was for sleeping, the other for cooking.

■ Cut doorways in **two shoeboxes**. Connect the boxes with **cardboard**. Cover with rolled **paper** or **craft sticks. Paint** brown. Mount to cardboard, add detail—corral, horses, cowboy bunkhouse.

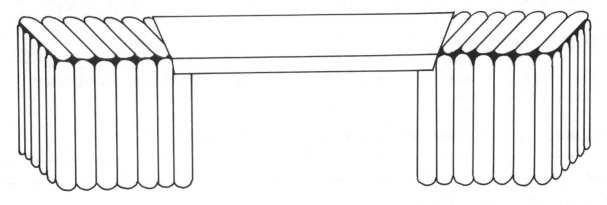

Miner's Rock House

A miner often slept outdoors in summer and built a **crude shack** in winter. He might have a tent or make a shelter out of rocks, empty boxes or packing cases lined with newspaper for warmth.

■ Cut an opening in a **plastic tub**. Cover with **small rocks** or pebbles—aquarium rock will work—held by **rubber** or **contact cement**. Line the inside with **newspaper** scraps. Mount on **cardboard**. Surround with detail—pick and ax, mining pan, gold nuggets, burro, claim stake.

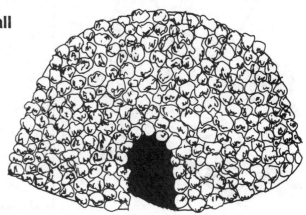

Pioneer Men

Dressed in Buckskin

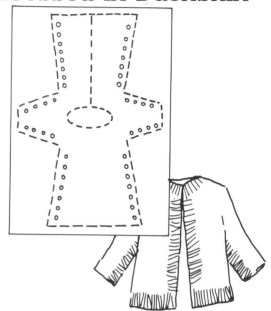

For early pioneer men in the Apalachian regions, just getting dressed was a difficult task. Clothes were made from deerskin stitched together with sinews from the animal. Once wet, buckskin dried as stiff as wood but was a good windbreaker and protected against thorns and snakes. Just imagine your pants standing up, waiting for you to get in!

Make a fringed buckskin shirt to wear:
• Use the illustration as a guide to cut a pattern from butcher paper. Measure from just below the waist, over the shoulder and back to the waist again to determine size.

• Cut as shown by the dotted lines.

• Punch holes as far as a hole punch will reach from the edge of the paper (as indicated by dots) every two inches.

• Match sides and holes, stitch with yarn or string. Fringe to the stitching.

Great Plains Garb

Men on the western frontier wore the same plain garments every day. A wool shirt, vest, felt hat, blue jeans (thanks to a man named Levi Strauss), boots, and an occasional pair of socks made up his wardrobe. He often wore a red bandana handkerchief around his neck to protect himself from dust and cold weather.

Check your closets at home. You might be surprised to find you too have levis and a red bandana in your wardrobe.

Experiment with a red handkerchief around the neck. Tie it in different ways (see pictures at left) then roleplay what you might be saying if you were a western pioneer wearing that bandana.

Pioneer Women

Historical Aid: The women who helped settle the frontier shared the same risks as the men. Life expectancy for these hard-working women was 38 to 40 years. They washed, cooked and baked with minimal supplies. They served as doctors for the ill and caretakers for the children. They spun their own wool and made all the clothing.

Their clothing was practical. Sunbonnets with wide brims protected their faces from the harsh sun. A simple calico or gingham dress was covered by an apron and a shawl was worn for warmth.

Make a sunbonnet and shawl and dress like a frontier woman.

Sunbonnet

Fold an 18" x 5" construction paper in half, lengthwise. Cut as shown by the dotted lines.

Fold a 16" x 14" piece of tissue paper in half lengthwise and cut as shown. Make several pleats in the curved edge of the tissue. Staple to the straight edge of the brim.

Pleat the bottom edge of the tissue and staple to a length of ribbon for tying under the chin.

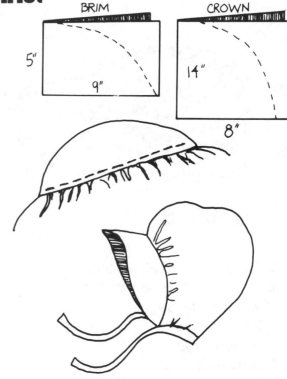

Shawl

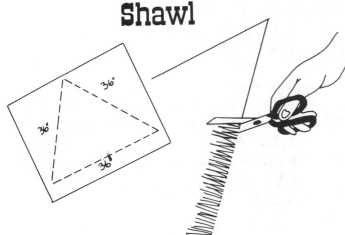

Cut a large triangle with three 36" sides from fabric or butcher paper. Fringe two sides. Tie around the shoulders.

Frontier Food

Historical Aid: Food on the frontier was simple. Flour was an important staple because it was nourishing and stored well. Flour was used in biscuits, bread and pancakes (called flapjacks).

Dried beans, game animals and preserved meats were also eaten. Rarely did frontiersmen eat fresh fruit, vegetables or dairy products.

Flapjacks

2 1/2 cups sifted all-purpose flour
6 teaspoons baking powder
2 tablespoons sugar
1 teaspoon salt
2 beaten eggs
2 cups milk
4 tablespoons salad oil

Sift together dry ingredients. Combine eggs, milk and oil. Add to dry mixture. Stir until flour is moistened (batter will be lumpy). Bake on hot griddle. Makes 24 dollar-size pancakes.

Biscuits

4 cups sifted all-purpose flour
6 teaspoons baking powder
1 teaspoon salt
1/2 cup shortening
2 cups milk

Cut shortening into sifted dry ingredients. Make a well in the center. Add milk. Stir quickly with a fork until dough follows fork around the bowl. Drop from teaspoon onto greased cookie sheet. Bake at 450°, 12-15 minutes. Makes 32 biscuits.

Historical Aid: Salt was extremely valuable to the pioneers. It was used for seasoning food and curing meat. But though salt was used extensively it was very difficult to obtain.

The Indians showed the settlers where to locate salt licks (springs). At the springs huge barrels were filled with water and placed over fires to boil and evaporate. Corn meal was added to the barrels to speed crystallization.

This job took days. 600 gallons of water had to be evaporated to yield one bushel of salt!

Salt Sampling

Make salt in your classroom.

If you live near a salt water supply, bring several buckets to class.

If you do not live near a body of salt water simply use tap water and add a box of salt. The results should be the same.

Measure the water and fill a large kettle. Place the kettle on a hot plate.

During the course of the day, observe the changing water level, discuss evaporation and add more water. Keep track of the quantity added. Children can take turns adding water, with adult supervision, of course.

When all the water has been evaporated (or the school day is over) measure the salt. Let each child sample a bit.

Frontier Recreation

Historical Aid: Almost any event on the frontier was turned into a contest. Men, women and children participated in apple paring, logrolling, cornhusking, wood chopping and spelling bees. Men often competed in a shooting match.

Children had their own games and toys, including homemade sleds and small wagons. Boys made bows, arrows and slings and became skilled in their use while enjoying target practice competition.

There was always plenty of food, fiddle-playing and dancing too!

Target Practice

Here are a couple target-practice variations. The slingshot should be made by older children and used only with CLOSE SUPERVISION. Discuss safety rules and usage before playing.

Make a target—on a large square of butcher paper. Paint four circular bands in different colors. Paint the center circle red. This is the bull's eye.

Younger children can throw a beanbag. Older students can toss a stone marked with chalk. That way, when the stone strikes the target it can be easily marked. Still older students can make a slingshot for their target practice.

To make a slingshot, ask kids to hunt for a forked twig in their yards. Tie a length of 1/4" elastic to each end of the forks. Collect small pebbles. Practice pulling back the elastic and shooting the pebble.
SHOOT ONLY AT THE TARGET NEVER NEAR OTHER STUDENTS.

Corn Husking

In the fall, corn had to be husked. Families gathered together in the evening for a husking bee. Your classroom husking bee will be during the day but use your imagination and picture yourself on the frontier!

Supply an ear of corn for each player. Cook it later for sampling. Choose two captains. Each captain chooses his team. Divide the corn evenly. Be sure there is an ear for each player on the team.

Frontier people sat shoulder to shoulder with a huge pile of corn in the center of their team. Your husking bee will be slightly different. Line the teams back to back. At a starting signal one player from each team picks an ear of corn and husks it. When finished he tags the next member, and so on.

After all ears have been husked, judge the ears to make sure they have been "husked clean!"

If a young settler found he had husked a red ear of corn, he could kiss the girl of his choice! (You may want to mark one red ear . . or several!)

Each man carried his own husking peg—a sharpened piece of wood, held in the palm of the hand by a leather strap that fit around the fingers. Make your own husking pegs by securing a golf tee to a rubber band. Slip it over the hand. You probably won't be able to use them as effectively as the pioneers but you'll understand their use.

Tell a Tale

Historical Aid: Storytelling was a popular leisure-time activity. As the stories were passed along from trail to trail and home to home, they became greatly exaggerated. Some were humorous while others told of courageous acts and daredevil deeds. Western adventurers, explorers, peace officers and outlaws alike became legendary due to this simple frontier recreation.

Here are some frontier tale activities:

Select a name from one of the lists and find out more. Do one of the following:
- Write a short report.
- Dress up as this person and tell your story to the class.
- Make a poster collage depicting three to five events in this person's life.

Use your imagination and make up your own frontier legend.
> Create a name.
> Tell why he or she is best remembered.
> Describe an amazing accomplishment.
> Write a physical description.

Leaders of the Westward Movement

Daniel Boone
Kit Carson
William Clark
Meriwether Lewis
Davy Crockett
Samuel Houston
Zebulon Montgomery Pike
Brigham Young
Sacajawea

Western Frontier Life

The Pioneers
Judge Roy Bean
Billy the Kid
Buffalo Bill Cody
Calamity Jane
Wyatt Earp
Wild Bill Hickock
Bat Masterson
Annie Oakley
Belle Starr

Other Western Legends

Sitting Bull
Geronimo
Paul Bunyan
Johnny Appleseed
Pecos Bill
Nat Love
Sequoyah

Important Invention

Historical Aid: Wood was scarce on the prairies and plains of the western frontier. Pioneer farmers planted thick, thorny shrubs instead of building fences to contain their livestock. The invention of barbed wire in 1873 was inspired by these thorned shrubs.

The idea was simple. Two or more steel wires were twisted together to create a barbed effect. This enabled farmers to fence in their homesteads and kept the free-roaming cattle off their property. Ranchers were not happy with the new invention because it brought an end to the open range.

It was due to this simple invention that the pioneers were able to settle the frontier and prosper.

Barbed Wire

Paint a picture that shows the effect that barbed wire had on the prairies and plains.

Create a wire effect by gluing a twisted line of black yarn or wire across the center of a large piece of drawing or construction paper. (If wire or yarn are not available, the same effect can be achieved with a thin line of black tempera paint.)

On one half, color or paint a farmer's homestead—house, chicken, horses, cattle.

On the other half sponge paint the grassy, open plains.

Historical Aid: Although wagons and horses were common forms of transportation on the frontier, most people traveled by stagecoach. A group could defend more easily than a lone rider against attacking Indians or bandits. Stagecoaches often carried strong boxes filled with precious cargo which made them prey to robbery.

The coaches covered 100 miles in 24 hours. Passengers, facing dust in the summer and cold in the winter, tried to sleep on hard seats as they bumped along. Wood or adobe stations were staggered every ten miles along the road providing travelers a chance to rest and stretch.

Stagecoach Activities

• Pretend you are a stagecoach driver. What is the precious cargo you are carrying? Draw a large rectangle on paper. This is the strongbox. Glue magazine pictures inside to show the precious cargo in your possession.

• Adapt the song "The Wheels on the Bus" to "The Wheels on the Coach" and make up your own verses. Example, "The driver on the coach says 'Giddyap horse.' "

• Place two chairs opposite two other chairs. These are the seats in a stagecoach. Put passengers in the coach. Roleplay the following situations:

   An Indian attack … a runaway stagecoach … a robbery

Frontier Transportation

The stagecoach was not the only other form of transportation used by the pioneers. Here are some other transportation activities.
• Find out about river travel. Build a *flatboat* using craft sticks with a boxed shelter in the middle. Make a model of the Erie Canal. Write a research paper about the canal.
• Find out about and describe the building of the first transcontinental *railroad*. Make a replica of the "Golden Spike." Reenact the moment that the golden spike completed the construction.

Historical Aid: Frontier townspeople depended a great deal on the work of the blacksmith. His job was to make and repair iron objects. First the iron was heated to a red glow and then hammered into shape by hand.

The most important item made by the frontier blacksmith was horseshoes to protect the feet of horses.

Use the pattern to trace and cut a horseshoe from tagboard.

Cover the horseshoe with crumpled foil. Press and "hammer" the foil into shape. Brush with black india ink.

Blacksmith

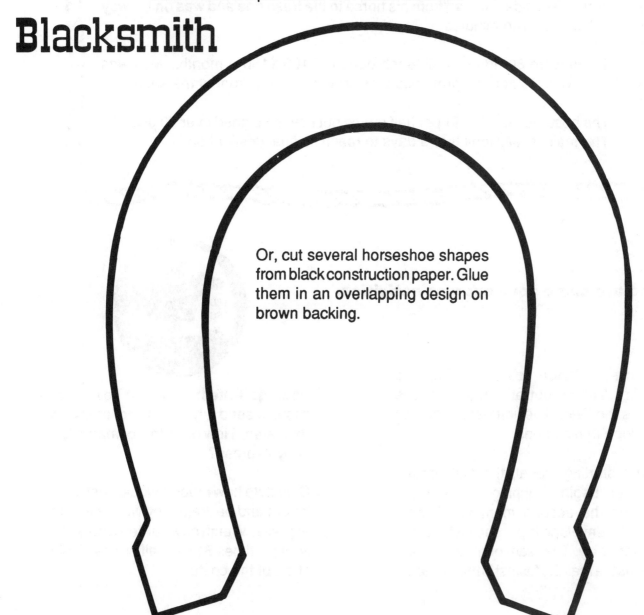

Or, cut several horseshoe shapes from black construction paper. Glue them in an overlapping design on brown backing.

The Pony Express

Historical Aid: The pony express was a service that transported mail by means of daring riders on horseback. The route began in St. Joseph, Missouri and traveled along the Oregon-California Trail. The riders braved rough trails, harsh weather and Indian attacks along their route that took them along the Platte River in Nebraska, south of the Great Salt Lake and across the Sierra Nevada Mountains to the final destination of Sacramento, California.

Pony express riders rode at top speed from one station to the next—about 75 miles. As the rider approached the station a keeper brought out a fresh horse. The rider jumped from his horse to the fresh one and was on his way in less than two minutes.

There were 80 riders in all, each earning $100-$150 a month. Mail was carried in leather, rainproof pouches strapped to the front ot the saddle.

The postage rate was $1 per half ounce but never weighed over 20 pounds. The mail usually took 8 or 9 days to reach its final destination.

Here are some pony express activities:

Station-to-station relay: Divide into teams. Spread out at equal distances across the field. The first person has an envelope in his hands.

At the starting signal, the first team member begins running. When he reaches the second member of the team the envelope is passed just like in a baton relay. The team of "riders" that passes the mail the fastest is the winner.

Postage Rates: Find out how much it costs to send a half ounce of mail at current rates. How does this compare to the pony express?

Calculate how much it would cost to send letters and packages by way of the pony express. Weigh several items on a scale. Multiply times $1 per half ounce. Make a chart of the costs.

Historical Aid: An average of 40 wagons banded together to form a wagon train heading west. Besides the elected positions among the passengers themselves, a wagon master and scout were hired to lead the way.

The wagon master was in charge. He made the final decisions, kept order on the trail, delegated responsibilities and ensured safe travel as best he could.

The scout traveled ahead to find water sources, locate hostile Indians and check for problems on the trail. He might be gone for days then rejoin the train and guide the way.

Scout and Wagon Master

Circle the Wagons

This was a familiar cry heard on the trail. At the end of each day of travel, or in the event of an Indian attack, the wagon master would lead the wagons into a large circle. This created a good windbreak and a defensive barricade.

The wagon master had to know just how large to make the circle so that the lead wagon closed the circle next to the last wagon.

Stand in a line with your classmates. The last person in line stands in place. The first person attempts to lead the "wagons" (the people in line) so that when he rejoins the last person a perfectly-sized circle is formed with all "wagons" standing a shoulder width apart.

Follow That Trail

A scout marked the trail for the wagon master to follow by bending down the branches of saplings.

Divide into pairs. One person is the scout the other is the wagon master.

The scout marks a trail using bent pipe cleaners or small twigs. The wagon master attempts to follow.

Where does the trail end—a lake, a grassy meadow?

Sheriff

Historical Aid: There were no courts or law officers in the early pioneer settlements. People needed to work together peacefully just to survive. But if problems arose they were usually solved—with fist and guns.

As towns developed on the western frontier, so did trouble with outlaws and robbers. Some towns hired a sheriff, also called a marshal, to enforce some order.

Being sheriff was dangerous and difficult. Most men carried weapons and fought freely on the streets. When someone committed a crime, a wanted poster appeared in frontier communities. Settlers armed themselves and rode after the outlaws themselves. An outlaw that was caught was shot or hanged.

Become sheriff for the day and write a wanted poster: Use the poster form (following) and include imaginary information. Here are some ideas:

WHO:
Big Bad John
Montana Joe
Crazy-Legs Willie
Sam "Buffalo" Snyder

WANTED FOR:
Horse thieven'
Cattle rustlin'
Cheatin' at cards
Stagecoach robbery
Train robbery

WHERE AND WHEN:
Tombstone
Abilene
Deadwood
Dry Gulch

Choose a date between 1850 and 1880

REWARD:
What amount could a pioneer earn by bringing in this outlaw?

DRAW a picture in the frame provided of the wanted man or woman.

WANTED

_____

_____

_____

_____

_____

_____

_____

_____

☆ **REWARD** ☆

$ _____

Sheriff _____

Brand-name Ranchers

Historical Aid: Cattle ranching was a major business on the frontier. Ranchers found they had to protect their cattle from being lost or stolen. Each rancher created a design called a **brand** from a combination of letters and symbols. The brand was registered with county or state authorities. The brand was burned into the cattle's skin as a form of identification.

Many ranches were also named after the brand. Some examples are:

Circle W Ranch

Box B Ranch

Broken Y Ranch

Pretend you own a cattle ranch on the frontier. Design a brand that will name your ranch and identify your cattle. You can use your initials or a combination of the symbols on the branding iron chart. You can change any of the symbols to suit your ideas. For example Crazy R can become Crazy M if your name begins with the letter "M".

After you have made a rough sketch of your brand use black or brown crayon to make the final drawing on a crumpled paper bag. Or use cut sponge or potatoes to make prints.

Register your brand. Reproduce the design on an index card and file it with the county "registrar." (This can be an elected or appointed position.)

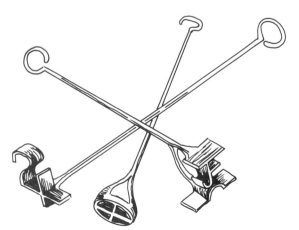

Branding Iron Chart

Rocking 7	Running W	Crazy R	Lazy R

Flying7	Hooked Y	Forked Y	Triple K

Bar	Double Bar	Broken Bar	Slash

Half Circle	Circle	Double Circle	Half Box

Double Box	Triangle	Diamond	Open A

Rocking Chair	Broken heart	Spur	Stirrup

Sunrise	Broken L	Tumbling R	Reverse R
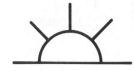			

Cowboy Collage

Historical Aid: A horse was a cowboy's most important possession. It was his only form of transportation and helped him earn a living. A cowboy had to be a good horseman as he lived in the saddle for many hours every day.

Rope was the cowboy's most important tool. He used it to catch cattle, hold his horse, pull wagons across muddy rivers, tie packs in place and kill snakes. Cowboys became adept with using a rope about 40 feet in length called a **lariat**.

Cowboys believed that if a rope was placed in a circle around a sleeping man it would protect him from snakes.

Make a cowboy collage that displays these two prized possessions.

On construction paper trace, sketch or glue a magazine picture of a horse.

Glue bits of rope or one length of rope in a circle around the horse.

Add scraps of bandana material, if available.

How the West Was Sung

Historical Aid: Cowboys spent many long, boring hours on the trail. They often sang songs to pass time and to soothe the herd.

Most often the words to a song were set to an existing tune. The song was then passed to others to be altered and added to. There could be a thousand verses. If a tune had more notes than the cowboy had words, he would sometimes hum or add nonsense words like "whoopee ti-yi-yo" until he could think of the next verse.

Here's a cowboy song to learn and sing together.

Get Along Little Doggies

As I was out walk-ing one morn-ing for pleas-ure, I spied a cow-punch-er a-rid-in' a-long. His hat was thrown back and his spurs were a-jing-lin', And as he ap-proached he was sing-in' this song: Whoo-pee Ti - Yi - Yo___ Git A-long Lit-tle Do-gies, it's your mis-for-tune and none of my___ own, Whoo-pee Ti - Yi - Yo, Git A-long Lit-tle Do-gies, you know that Wy-o-ming will be your new home.

Cowboy Clothing

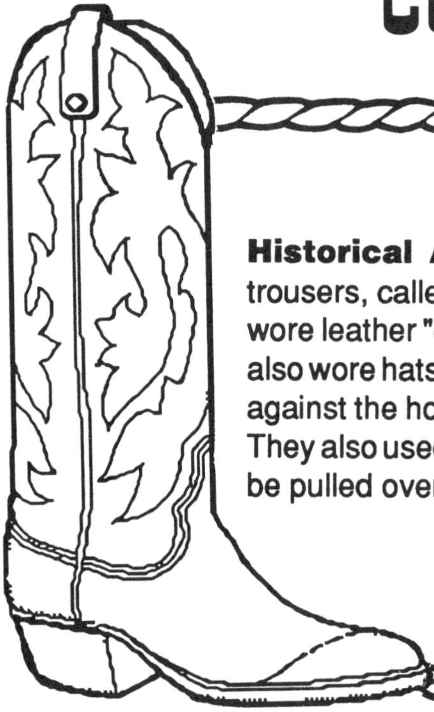

Historical Aid: Clothing was very simple and practical—boots, trousers, called *levis*, a wool shirt, jacket or vest and a hat. Cowboys wore leather "chaps" to protect their legs from prickly sagebrush. They also wore hats called sombreros that had a wide brim to shield their eyes against the hot sun and a deep crown to keep the hat from blowing off. They also used their hats as a bucket! A bandana around the neck could be pulled over his face as a filter against dust.

Chaps

From brown butcher paper, cut two shapes, like those shown at right, the length of your leg.

Cut a 2" strip large enough to fit around your waist and staple the leggings to the waistband.

Add yarn to each side of the legging bottom so the chaps can be secured around the ankle.

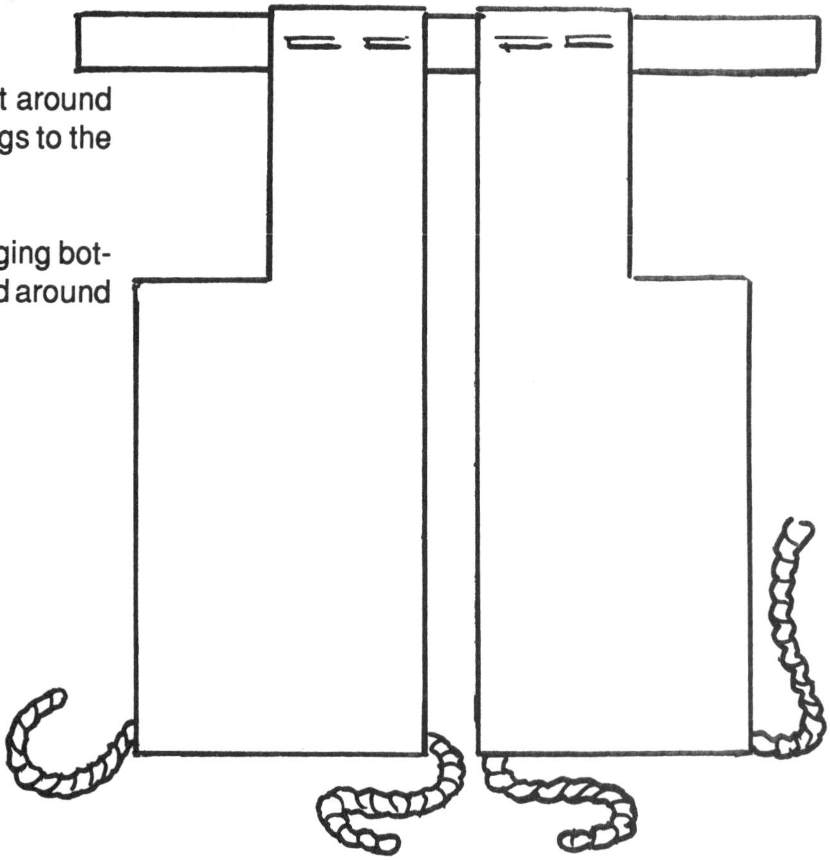

Ten Gallon Hat

Could a hat really hold ten gallons of water?

Try this experiment.

Ask kids to bring a hat to class. (It must be able to get wet!).
Measure ten gallons of water into a large tub.
Mark the water level on the tub.
Let each child measure the amount of water his or her hat will hold.
Keep refilling the tub to the ten-gallon mark.

Compare the results. Which hat held the most? the least?

Were any hats able to hold ten gallons? Would the children like to rename the famous Texas hat?

Historical Aid: Cowboys on a long cattle drive worked up huge appetites and cooking from a wagon was a difficult task. Colonel Charles Goodnight of Texas invented a wagon that helped make work easier for the cattle drive cook.

A large box was built in the back of an ordinary wagon. It had a hinged door that served as a work table when lowered. Inside there were storage shelves.

The chuck wagon stocked pots, pans, tin cups and eating utensils. The storage box was filled with sugar, coffee beans, bacon, lard and sourdough starter for making hearty biscuits.

Chuck Wagon

Set up a chuck wagon kitchen in your classroom. A card table or desk will work fine. Discuss what food items your "cowboys" and "cowgirls" would like to stock in their chuckwagon. Kids can bring in empty, cleaned cans, flour bags, sugar tins and so on. They can cut pictures from magazines and glue them to cardboard to help stock the shelves.

Once the chuck wagon is stocked children can plan meals to serve on the cattle drive. Younger children can set aside the ingredients and explain their menu.

Ask older students to create a chuck wagon meal—breakfast, lunch or dinner. The ingredients must be found in your classroom chuck wagon. Write the menus on plain paper, tear the edges and post the menus around the chuck wagon.

Lunch
beans
slaw
biscuits
coffee

Canned Goods

Historical Aid: Cowboys of the old west had little opportunity to read. There just wasn't a lot of available material, so they practiced by reading labels on canned food.

Around a campfire they tried to recite word for word (with commas, periods, etc.) everything on a can label. This became a game called "know your cans."

Can Creativity

Invent a new product and give it an old west name such as "round up ravioli" or "branding iron beans."

Using an empty can to measure the size, create a label for your product. Refer to real can labels to see what information needs to be on it. Tape the new label on the can.

With a partner, play your own game of "know your cans." Take time to study your cans, then alternate trying to recite and spell all the words.

Enrichment

Set up a store with the cans you created or with other cans brought in. Research to see what other items might have been sold in a small frontier shop. Make your store as authentic as possible with real items or pictures.

Research to find out what the prices may have been then and put price tags on items. How much money might it cost to feed a cowboy for a week? How much would your family have to spend for groceries at this store?

Rodeo Day Roundup

Historical Aid: Twice a year, cowboys from as many as ten ranches rounded up the cattle on the open range and herded them to a central place. Here they sorted the cattle according to their brands and branded all new calves.

This roundup was both a time for work and a social event. As many as 300 cowboys participated in an athletic contest called a rodeo after their work was finished.

The men competed in bare back riding, steer wrestling, calf roping and other tests of skill. They also gathered to share stories, sing songs and make music.

It is believed that the first rodeo ever held for spectators other than the participating cowboys was in Pecos, Texas in 1883.

Enjoy a day devoted to the rodeo in your classroom. Involve students in the planning. Read the suggested activities that follow and choose those they would like to try.

Calf Roping

Actual: Cowboy and horse work together to lasso a calf, throw it to the ground and tie three legs together.

Rodeo Day: Play tug-of-war with shortened ropes. A cowboy and a horse are one side, two "calves" are on the other.

Steer Wrestling

Actual: Rider jumps from a horse onto a steer back and wrestles it to the ground in a timed contest.

Rodeo Day: A player holding the pillow is the steer. The "cowboy" tries to wrestle the pillow from the steer and throw it to the ground.

Bronco Riding

Actual: Rider must remain mounted for eight seconds on a bucking bronco.

Rodeo Day: Who can stay on a pogo stick for eight seconds? (Or jump the most times?)

Have some fun with brands...

● Play this version of pin the tail on the donkey. Tack a large picture of a cow on the wall. Mark a spot on the cattle's hind side. Supply a blindfold and a brand. Who can come closest to the spot?

Round 'em Up

● Create enough brands on brown-bag squares so that every player has one. There should be three to six different brands but the quantity of each does not have to be the same. Put a strip of double-sided tape on the back of each brand.

All the "cattle" groups together. At a signal players look for others with the same brand and divide into groups. How quickly can they accomplish this?

As a variation, two "cowboys" can sort the "cattle" by brand. Time them. Then give two more cowboys a chance to beat that time.

Rope Tricks

• Play a version of "horse-shoes" but use a rope ring, instead. (Or play horseshoes!)

• Learn how to tie some different knots with a length of rope.

And as the sun settles ... try these quiet cowboy activities—

• Learn to sing "Home on the Range" or "Red River Valley."
• Listen to true-life stories or biographies about legendary old west adventurers. Bring some library books for some free-time reading.
• Listen to the callers on a square dancing record ... or see a movie. Learn a few square dancing steps.

Cowboy Beans

2 lb. pinto beans	4 Tbsp sugar
2 lb. ham hock	2 green chiles, chopped
2 chopped onions	1 can tomato paste

Wash beans and soak overnight. Place beans in a crockpot or Dutch oven and cover with water. Add remaining ingredients. Cook until beans are tender.

Have you worked up a "prairie-sized" appetite?

Rustle up some **Cowboy Beans**.

Boom Town

Historical Aid: Frontier towns seemed to be built overnight as centers for cattle transporting, mining and shipping. these instant towns were called boom towns. There were few comforts in these boom towns. Many homes were built from rocks, bottles or packing cases. The towns were dusty and often filled with more cattle than people.

Main street buildings were built in a hurry too. Many were simple frame structures with false fronts.

The first cattle town was built in 1867 in Abilene, Kansas. The last was the busiest—Dodge City, Kansas. There were, however, many more towns scattered across the west.

Each student can contribute to the construction of "Main Street" in a western boom town.

Cut a simple store front from tagboard, construction paper, or a cereal box. Glue the store front shape to the end of a shoebox. Add detail—windows, door, sign.

Some of the buildings found in a boom town were:

Saloon	Hotel
Town Hall	Telegraph Office
Barber	Boarding House
General Store	Asseyors Office
Blacksmith	

Assemble all the buildings and place them side by side. Children may want to add more to the town—stick sidewalks, raffia tumbleweeds, hitching posts etc. They can also create dioramas depicting the business.

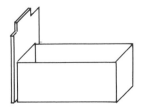